KU-531-635

FULL CIRCLE
THE PHOTOGRAPHS

FOR **PATRICA** AND **SONIA**

FULL CIRCLE
THE PHOTOGRAPHS

PHOTOGRAPHY & DESIGN BY BASIL PAO
INTRODUCTION BY MICHAEL PALIN

BBC BOOKS

617934

MORAY COUNCIL
Department of Technical
& Leisure Services
910.4

This book is published to accompany the television series *Full Circle,* produced by
Prominent Television and Passpartout Productions for the BBC, first broadcast on
BBC1 in 1997. Series producer: Clem Vallance. Producer/Director: Roger Mills.
Executive producer for Prominent: Anne James. Executive producer for BBC:
Edward Mirzoeff. All photographs by Basil Pao. Copyright © Basil Pao 1997.
Introduction © Michael Palin 1997. Published by BBC Books, an imprint of BBC
Worldwide Publishing. BBC Worldwide Limited, 80 Wood Lane, London W12
OTT. First published 1997. The moral right of the author has been asserted. All
rights reserved. No part of this publication may be reproduced, stored in a
retrieval system, or transmitted in any form or by any means, electronic,
mechanical, photocopying, recording, or otherwise, without written permission
from the copyright holder and the publisher. ISBN 0 563 37168 4. Produced and
designed in Hong Kong by Basil Pao with Lillian Tang Design Ltd. Printed and
bound in Great Britain by Butler and Tanner Ltd, Frome and London. Jacket
printed by Lawrence Allen Ltd, Weston-super-Mare. Colour reproduction by
Radstock Reproductions Ltd. Midsomer Norton.

ABOVE ▪ Rain over the Perfume River, Hue, Vietnam.
PRECEDING PAGES ▪ El Tatio, the highest geyser field in the world. Chile.
OVERLEAF ▪ Lake Titicaca, Bolivia.

12

Sunset over the Last Hope Sound outside Puerto Natales. Provincia del Ultimo Esperanza, Chile.

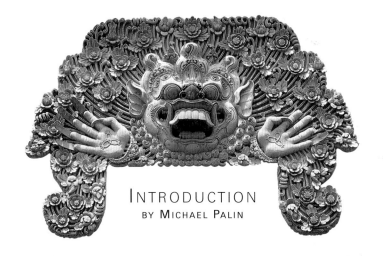

INTRODUCTION
BY MICHAEL PALIN

The Pacific Ocean covers one-third of the world's surface and around it lives one-third of the world's population. Its seventy million square miles of water spill onto the shores of a rich and diverse assortment of countries. Some are global giants – Russia, China, Japan and The United States all have Pacific coastlines – others, such as Korea, Malaysia, Indonesia, Australia, New Zealand, Chile and Canada are, or are becoming, increasingly important and influential. The shores of the Pacific have long been a geomorphic entity, The Ring of Fire, bristling with volcanoes and split by constant earthquakes. Now the countries with coastline on this vast ocean are growing into a political and economic entity. They call it the Pacific Rim.

Experts predict that the Pacific Rim will be the powerhouse of the twenty-first century. Flushed with millennial zeal, Western commentators point to the final decline of the Mediterranean-Atlantic axis which has dominated the world for the past two thousand years. The future, we are told, belongs to the other side of the earth. The Pacific century is about to begin. As if to emphasize the potency of this change, the predatory wresting away of the Western initiative, the Pacific economies are likened to ferocious animals – tigers, dragons and the like. Fortunes are once again being won or lost beside the shark-infested waters of the South-East Pacific. More and more of what we eat, wear, listen to or watch is produced on the Pacific. More and more Western tourists are prepared to make the long journey out there. The Pacific Rim is a fact of life.

But do any of us actually know what the Pacific Rim consists of, which countries it is made up of and how far it stretches?

When myself, my film crew and photographer Basil Pao set out in walrus skin boats from the tiny isolated island of Little Diomede in the Bering Strait, we were, as far as I know, the first people who had ever set out to attempt a full circle of the Pacific Rim. We travelled for 50,000 miles and filmed for the best part of a year, returning home briefly to do some laundry and save our marriages.

The Pacific Rim is the most geomorphically active area in the world. It is at the edge of a remorseless grinding confrontation between the bed of the ocean and the great Continental land-masses. The resulting stresses and strains and folds and splits have created achingly beautiful landscapes which

ABOVE ▪ Temple doorway. Lombok Island, Indonesia.

LEFT ▪ Michael Palin in Wushan, the easternmost city of Sichuan Province on the Yangtze River, China.

often proved impossible to cross – giant cul-de-sacs from which there would have been no access before the invention of the helicopter. We circled volcanic craters high on the Kamchatka Peninsula, crossed bleak and desolate Siberian wastelands to the remains of a Gulag prison camp, flew out of the clouds onto the human anthill of a Colombian emerald mine and took a float plane to a remote breeding ground of brown bears in the Aleutian Islands. We relied on canoes to take us up the headwaters of the Amazon and the backwaters of Borneo, trains to take us down the coast of Vietnam, across the bleached deserts of central Australia and through the forests of British Columbia, and creaking old ferries to carry us through the Yangtze gorges and across the perilous seas south of the Philippines. We travelled through eighteen countries and filmed and photographed for two hundred and fifty days.

There were many times in that year in the Pacific when resources ran low and the whole effort seemed overwhelming. But, as with the best journeys, this was often because there was no let-up in the sheer richness of what we saw and experienced. It was a journey of dazzling surprises and jarring extremes. Beauty and ugliness, sophistication and squalor, unceasing urban noise and monastic tranquillity, Los Angeles freeways and Amazonian rapids, shrieking winds on icy glaciers 16,000 feet high, and the serenity of coral reefs 100 feet deep. There was not a single day when we did not see something remarkable.

It is to Basil Pao's credit that so many of these revelations are captured in this book. For Basil, who produced *Pole to Pole: The Photographs* this was an opportunity he could not miss and did not waste. A constantly changing gallery of experiences, a year long parade of the world's most striking faces and places.

This book means a lot to me because I saw what Basil saw as we circled the Pacific together but, as with *Pole to Pole*, he added another dimension to the journey. He has given the extraordinary and fleeting a permanence. He has caught beauty in a single glance and captured moments I thought had gone forever.

Full Circle: The Photographs is the best of the best. This is the Pacific Rim, illuminated.

ABOVE ▪ Door god from the *Kraton*, the eighteenth-century palace of the Sultans of Yogyakarta. Central Java, Indonesia.

RIGHT ▪ Yoshi Kazu, an original founder of the Kodo drummers, performing a solo on the *O-daiko* in Maki, Japan.

PETROPAVLOV
KAMCHATKA PENINSULA
MAGADAN
VLADIVOSTOK
TOYAMA
NIIGATA
SADO ISLAND
MAKI
KUROHIME
TOKYO
MIHARA
HIROSHIMA
NAGASAKI
HAKATA
PUSAN
KYONGJU
SEOUL
PANMUNJOM
INCHON
QINGDAO
TAI'AN
SHANGHAI
YICHANG
WUSHAN
CHONGQING
GUIYANG
NANNING
DONG DANG
HANOI
HUE
DA NANG
SAIGON
BANAUE
BAGUIO
MANILA
DAVAO
SAMAL ISLAND
GENERAL SANTOS
ZAMBOANGA
SANDAKAN
KUCHING
SARAWAK
JAKARTA
BANDUNG
YOGYAKARTA
BOROBUDUR
BROMO
SURABAYA
BALI
LOMBOK
DARWIN
KATHERINE
ALICE SPRINGS
KING'S CANYON
ADELAIDE
SYDNEY
AUCKLAND
WELLINGTON
PICTON
KAIKOURA
CHRISTCHURCH
MT COOK
DUNEDIN
QUEENST

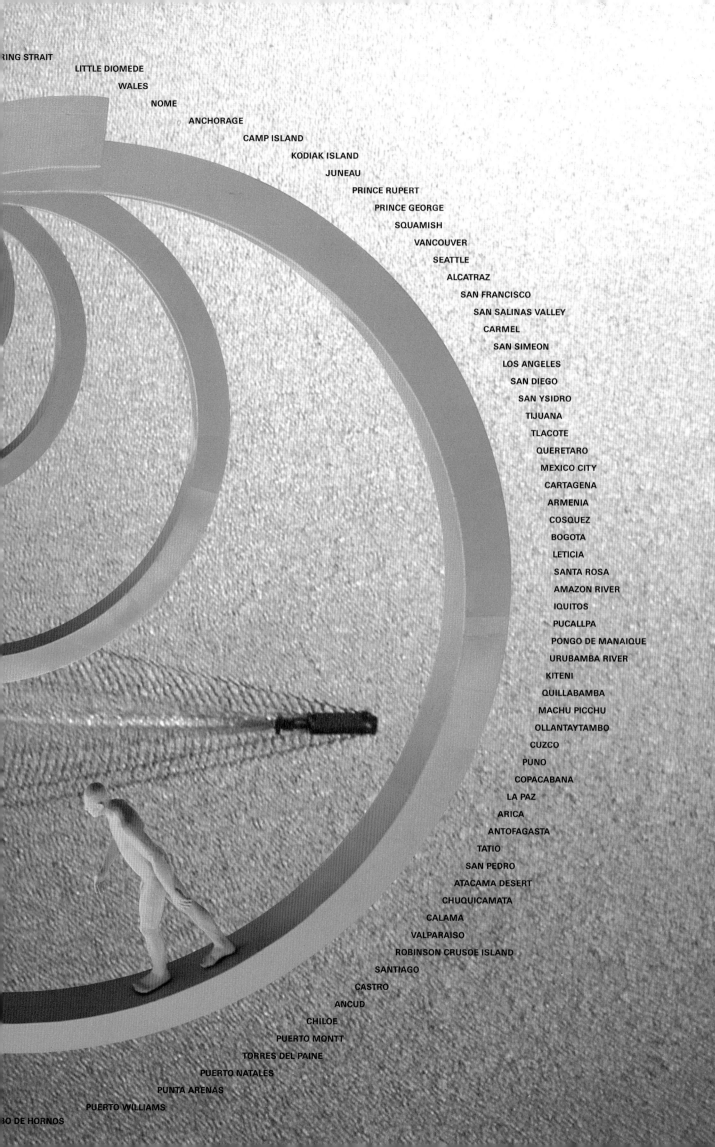

RING STRAIT

LITTLE DIOMEDE

WALES

NOME

ANCHORAGE

CAMP ISLAND

KODIAK ISLAND

JUNEAU

PRINCE RUPERT

PRINCE GEORGE

SQUAMISH

VANCOUVER

SEATTLE

ALCATRAZ

SAN FRANCISCO

SAN SALINAS VALLEY

CARMEL

SAN SIMEON

LOS ANGELES

SAN DIEGO

SAN YSIDRO

TIJUANA

TLACOTE

QUERETARO

MEXICO CITY

CARTAGENA

ARMENIA

COSQUEZ

BOGOTA

LETICIA

SANTA ROSA

AMAZON RIVER

IQUITOS

PUCALLPA

PONGO DE MANAIQUE

URUBAMBA RIVER

KITENI

QUILLABAMBA

MACHU PICCHU

OLLANTAYTAMBO

CUZCO

PUNO

COPACABANA

LA PAZ

ARICA

ANTOFAGASTA

TATIO

SAN PEDRO

ATACAMA DESERT

CHUQUICAMATA

CALAMA

VALPARAISO

ROBINSON CRUSOE ISLAND

SANTIAGO

CASTRO

ANCUD

CHILOE

PUERTO MONTT

TORRES DEL PAINE

PUERTO NATALES

PUNTA ARENAS

PUERTO WILLIAMS

BO DE HORNOS

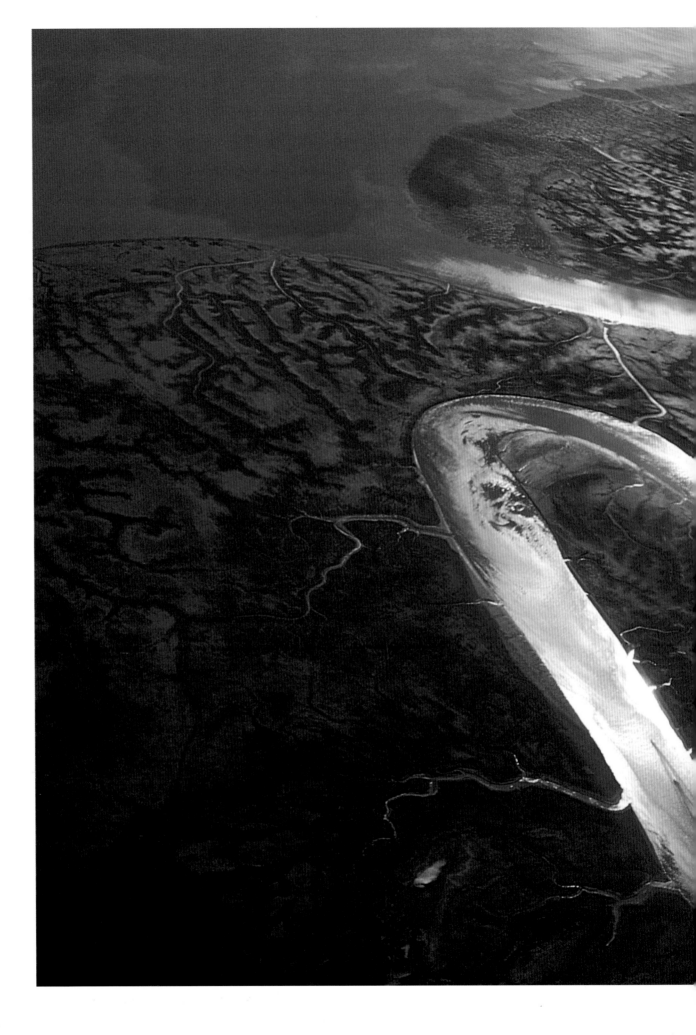

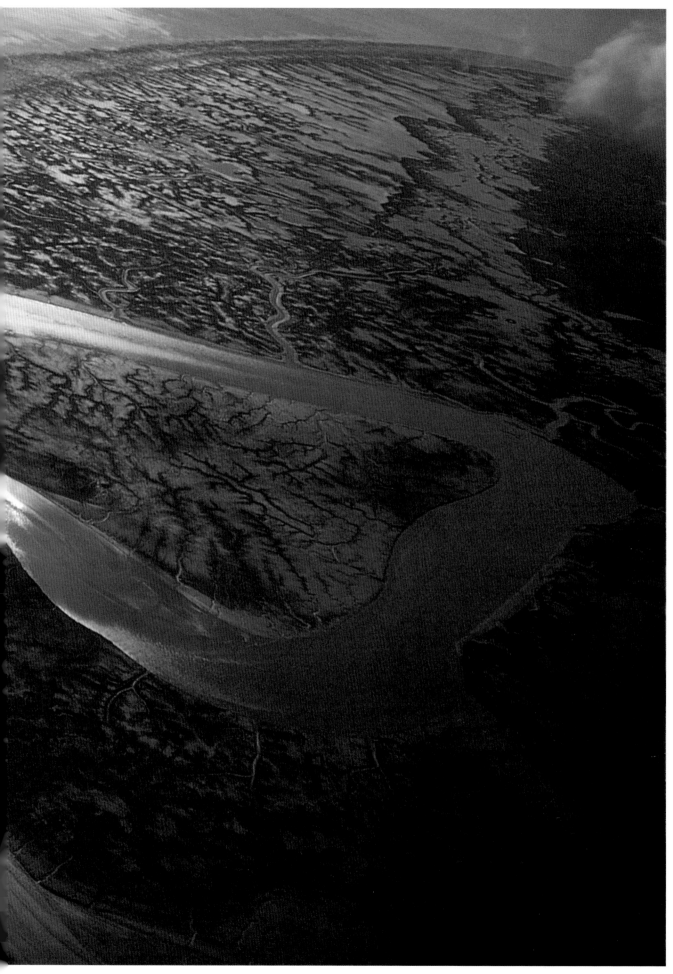

The Seward Peninsula on the Pacific coast of northern Alaska.

22

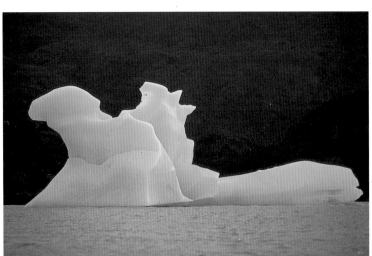

LAND

Storm over the Arnhem Land plateau, between the Victoria River and Katherine. Northern Territory, Australia.

PRECEDING PAGE ▪ Seven thousand year-old ice on Lago Grey. Torres del Paine National Park, Chile.

LEFT ▪ King Island, off the Pacific coast of northern Alaska.

Torres del Paine National Park, Provincia del Ultimo Esperanza, Chile.

Thunder storm over the Timor Sea. Darwin, Northern Territory, Australia.

Lago Grey glacier. Torres del Paine National Park, Provincia del Ultimo Esperanza, Chile.

ABOVE ▪ Torres del Paine National Park, Provincia del Ultimo Esperanza, Chile.

RIGHT ▪ The Alaskan Marine Highway outside Juneau, Alaska.

Tasman glacier, Mount Cook range. Southern Alps, New Zealand.

Torres del Paine mountains. Provincia del Ultimo Esperanza, Chile.

Train across the Andes, from Arica on the Pacific coast of Chile to La Paz in Bolivia, the highest capital in the world.

Prince Rupert Sound. British Columbia, Canada.

The Amazon River, Peru.

The Yukon River, Alaska.

Kronotsky Nature Reserve. Kamchatka, Russian Far East.

Torres del Paine National Park. Chile.

Caldera of the Uzon volcano. Kronotsky Nature Reserve. Kamchatka, Russian Far East.

Valley of the Geysers. Kronotsky Nature Reserve. Kamchatka, Russian Far East.

Valle de la Luna. Valley of the Moon in the Atacama desert, Chile.

One of the twenty-five volcanos within the Kronotsky Nature Reserve, Kamchatka, Russian Far East.

The Sacred Valley in the Andes, between Cuzco and Macchu Picchu, Peru.

The flooded plains of Luzon outside Manila, Philippines.

The Andes from 30,000 feet in the air. Chile.

Kronotsky Nature Reserve. Kamchatka, Russian Far East.

Mount Pinatubo, central Luzon, Philippines.

RIGHT ■ Agricultural plain of central Luzon, Philippines.

PRECEEDING PAGES ■ The Valley of Death, outside the town of San Pedro. Atacama desert, northern Chile.

The La Raya Pass, watershed of the Andes, from the train to Cuzco, Peru.

54

Lake Titicaca at Puno, Peru.

A riverboat on the Amazon river near the town of Caballococha in Peru.

Puerto Natales at daybreak. Provincia del Ultimo Esperanza, Chile.

Along the La Raya Pass from the train to Cuzco, Peru.

Japanese tourist at Machu Picchu, Peru.

62

PEOPLE

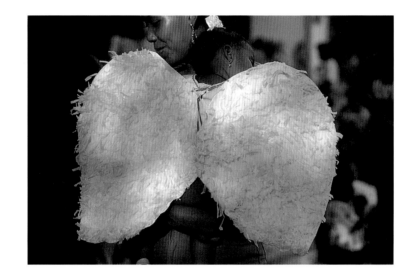

Miao minority outside Guiyang, Guizhou province, southern China.

RIGHT ▪ Mother and child at the train station in Julliaca, Peru.

PRECEEDING PAGES ▪ Mother and child in Cartagena, Columbia.

A street stall selling dried llama foetuses and other local medicines in La Paz, Bolivia.

LEFT ■ Child on the platform at Chongqing station. Sichuan province, China.

OVERLEAF ■ Children from the Rio Hondo, a Muslim city on stilts in Zamboanga. Mindanao, Philippines.

A descendant of the Incas. Ollantaytambo in the Sacred Valley, Peru.

Little drummer boy in a local folk festival. Chongqing, Sichuan, China.

A future *Aymara* boat-builder on the southern shores of Lake Titicaca, Bolivia.

Direct descendants of the Incas in a hill village above Ollantaytambo in the Sacred Valley, once the bread basket of the Inca empire. Peru.

An abandoned factory in Yelizovo, outside Petropavlovsk. Kamchatka, Russian Far East.

74

Boys from the village of Shimeng. Guizhou province, China.

Machiguenga boy in the jungle village of Shivankoreni, on the Camisea River in the Peruvian Amazon.

In the village of Shimeng, Guizhou province, China.

Kuching, Sarawak, Borneo.

78

ABOVE ▪ *Guaceros* – scavengers picking through the leftovers, downstream from the richest
emerald mine in the world – Cosquez, Boyaca Valley, Columbia

RIGHT ▪ Water delivery service at the Urubamba River, Sepahua, Peru.

Aboriginal settlement of Manyallaluk. Eva Valley, Northern Territory, Australia.

On the steps of the basilica of San Francisco. La Paz, Bolivia.

Outside Fort Pilar. Zamboanga, Philippines.

Outside Plaza de Armas, in 'the navel of the world' – Cuzco, Peru.

Bus terminal. Mexico City, Mexico.

Ocelot kitten for sale by the banks of the Amazon River, Peru.

Homework in Saigon, Vietnam.

Playground in Magadan, Russian Far East.

Carnival in the barrios of Santiago, Chile.

ABOVE ▪ Playground in Wellington, North Island, New Zealand.

LEFT ▪ The ferry crossing at San Pablo Tiquina. Lake Titicaca, Bolivia.

90

The Compass Cup – the world's only cow race. Mt Compass, South Australia.

RIGHT ■ The Maori challenge. Kaikoura, South Island, New Zealand.

PRECEDING PAGES ■ The Leith run. University of Otago. Dunedin, South Island, New Zealand.

Crewman on the *Oriental Jewel*, a passenger ferry on the Yangtze River. Sichuan province, China.

Kodo apprentice, Sado island, Japan.

After the Leith run. Dunedin, New Zealand.

Cartagena, Columbia.

Valparaíso, Chile.

Qingdao, China.

Soldier on the beach at Sepahua, guarding againest *narcos* and *contrabandidos*. Urubamba river, Peruvian Amazon.

U.S. Coastguard adjusting the rapid-fire cannon on board *U.S.C.G.C. Munro*. Bering Strait, Alaska.

On board the Chilean Navy frigate, *Izaza*. Cape Horn, Chile.

Remains of the Russian Pacific Fleet. Vladivostok, Russian Far East.

Makeshift grave in Butugychag, a forced labour camp at the uranium mines 150 miles north of Magadan. Russian Far East.

ABOVE ▪ The Peace Dome – Hiroshima Prefectural Industrial Promotion Hall. Hiroshima, Japan.

OVERLEAF ▪ A veteran from the Afghan war. Magadan, Russian Far East.

Blind musician outside the old palace. Its five-hundred-year-old limestone foundation a living reminder of the heyday of the Inca Empire. Cuzco, Peru.

Tatio geyser field in the Andes, northern Chile.

Coal worker in Wushan. Sichuan, China.

Cuzco, Peru.

Mount Bromo. Java, Indonesia.

Hue, Vietnam.

Armenia, Columbia.

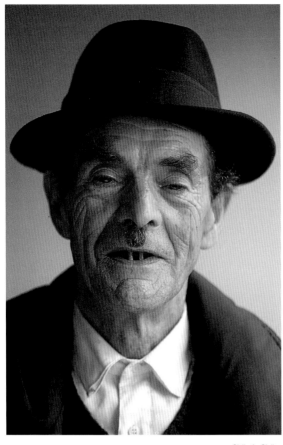

Chiloé, Chile.

Wushan. Sichuan, China.

Kuching, Sarawak, Borneo.

Nagasaki, Japan.

Shivankoreni, Peruvian Amazon.

Cartagena, Columbia

Queenstown, New Zealand.

Huis ten Bosch, Japan.

Magadan, Russian Far East.

Saigon, Vietnam.

Yoyogi park. Tokyo, Japan.

Mexican youth waiting to cross the fence into U.S.A. Tijuana, Mexico.

American youth out on the frontier. Nome, Alaska.

Sanitation worker in Nome, Alaska.

Wedding guest in Vladivostok, Russian Far East.

'Super Barrio'. Mexico City, Mexico.

Passenger onboard the *Oriental Star*, Yangtze River, China.

Querétaro, Mexico.

Qingdao, China.

Qingdao, China.

124

Saigon, Vietnam.

La Paz, Bolivia.

Perfume River, Hue, Vietnam.

Sado Island, northern Japan.

Passenger on board a Yangtze River ferry, China.

Villager from the Tengger Highlands, Java, Indonesia.

Machiguenga village elder. Shivankoreni, Camisea River, Peruvian Amazon.

Querétaro, Mexico.

Mount Bromo, Java, Indonesia.

Shivankoreni villager fishing on the Camisea River, Peruvian Amazon.

134

Paulino Esteban, Aymara master boatbuilder at work. Lake Titicaca, Bolivia.

Aboriginal artist outside Alice Springs, Australia.

Shipyard in Wushan by the Yangtze River. Sichuan province, China.

Cao Dai temple, Tay Ninh, south Vietnam.

Jeepney factory, Manila, Philippines.

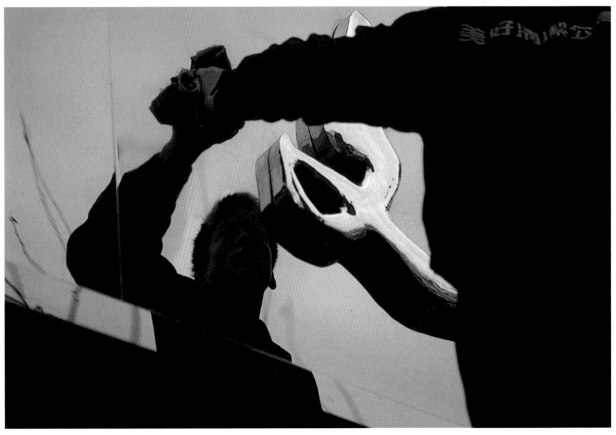

Bank entrance on Nanjing Road, Shanghai, China.

Iban Longhouse, Nanga Sumpa, Sarawak, Borneo.

Jeepney factory, Manila, Philippines.

Iban fisherman on the Sumpa River. Sarawak, Borneo.

Fisherman on Lombok Island, Indonesia.

Salt seller in Zamboanga, Mindanao, Philippines.

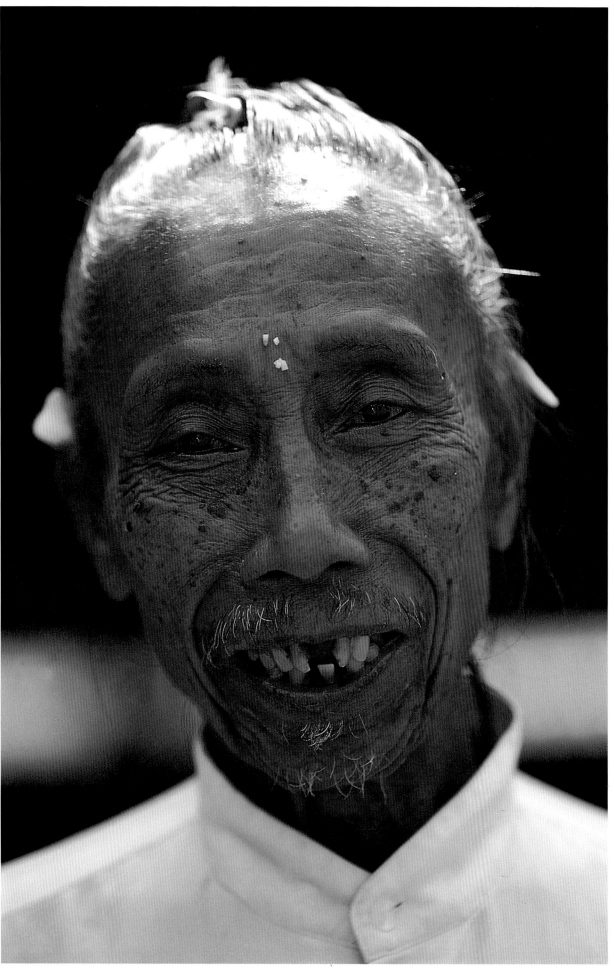

Temple priest, Lombok Island, Indonesia.

An Inaluk Eskimo carving out strips of beluga whale. Little Diomede Island, Bering Strait.

Market on the banks of the Urubamba River, Pucallpa, Peruvian Amazon.

Feast day at the Iban Longhouse. Nanga Sumpa, Sarawak, Borneo.

Procession in Plaza de Armas. Cuzco, Peru.

150

The cathedral in the border town of Copacabana, Bolivia.

The cruise ship *Oriana* docked in Sydney, Australia.

Saigon, Vietnam.

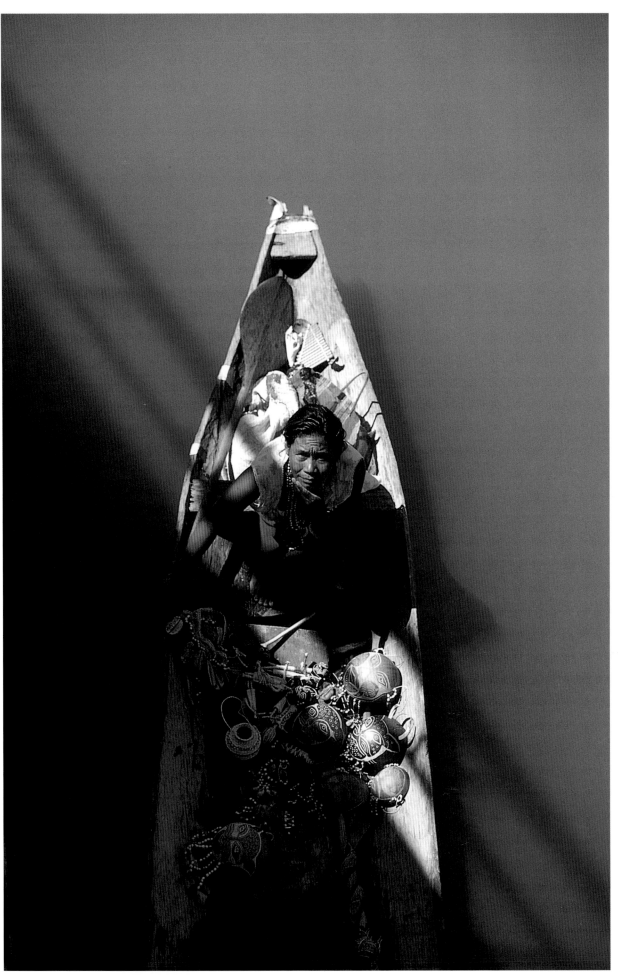

Amazon River, Peru.

ABOVE ▪ Cartagena, Columbia.

LEFT ▪ La Paz, Bolivia.

Santiago, Chile.

Magadan, Russian Far East.

RIGHT ■

Train station at Puno, Peru.

Cuzco, Peru.

Indian child selling trinkets on the Amazon River, Peru.

Shopping in the barrio of Belen, Iquitos, Peru.

Llama skin for sale at the Julliaca train station, Peru.

Hawker in Kyongju, South Korea.

Expulsion of the hawkers. Julliaca station, Peru.

A bar in Vinà del Mar, Valparaíso, Chile.

Woodman's hut in the Kronotsky Nature Reserve, Kamchatka, Russian Far East.

Money changer in Cuzco, Peru.

Ceiling of a bar in San Salinas, California, USA.

168

The strawberry fields of San Salinas, California, USA.

PRECEDING PAGES ■ An illegal immigrant who has literally one foot inside the U.S., through a crack in the *Tortilla Curtain*, Tijuana, Mexico.

RIGHT ■ On the banks of the Urubamba River, Peruvian Amazon.

Castro district, San Francisco, USA.

Chongqing, Sichuan province, China.

View outside the Ping-Hu hotel window. Yichang, China.

In the barrio of Belen, Iquitos, Peruvian Amazon.

176

177

Miao village outside Guiyang, Guizhou province, China.

Rice terraces outside Guiyang, Guizhou province, China.

Ploughing the flooded terraces outside Guiyang, Guizhou province, China.

Fifteen hundred-year-old rice terraces of Banaue, Luzon, Philippines.

Central Java, Indonesia.

'Will you buy me some new shoes?' Guizhou province, China.

Shimeng village outside Guiyang, Guizhou province, China.

Rice field in the Mekong River delta, south Vietnam.

Road to Guiyang, Guizhou province, China.

186

Cabbage patch on the hillsides of Mount Bromo, Java, Indonesia.

Pyramid of the Moon at Teotihuacan outside Mexico City, Mexico.

Procession of pilgrims at Bukit Gumang, a sacred hill on the east coast of Bali, Indonesia.

RIGHT ■ Procession of wild camels at King's Creek, Northern Territory, Australia.

OVERLEAF ■ Cartagena, Columbia.

The Zen temple at Buttsuji. Honshu Island, Japan.